MARY, TEACH ME TO PRAY

Life Is Fleeting

Eternity Is Forever

PRAY!   PRAY!   PRAY!

✢ ✢ ✢ ✢ ✢ ✢ ✢ ✢ ✢ ✢ ✢

DEDICATION

To Mary we dedicate this booklet of prayers. She has repeatedly said: "Pray! You have to pray!" It is our hope you will find these prayers useful and that you will heed Mary's words: "Pray, dear children. Pray from your heart." We urge you to listen to Her call, to hear Her request. It will be your gateway to eternal salvation.

MARY'S CALL
P.O. Box 162
504 W. U.S. Hwy. 24
Salisbury, MO 65281

Phone: 660-388-5308
Email: maryscall@maryscall.com

www.maryscall.com

MARY'S CALL

Mary's Call is a small, not-for-profit family organization. Our ministry is to encourage prayer, especially the Rosary and Way of the Cross.

The original undertaking of Mary's Call was the production of a 15 decade Rosary tape with meditations plus six hymns. The first order for the tape was received on May 4, 1989 (Ascension Thursday).

We create Mary's Call unique books and have available bibles, rosaries, scapulars, religious books, plaques, and many other items and religious gifts. In order for items to be sold at the lowest price, every effort is made to keep production costs to a minimum and, at the same time, maintain exceptional standards.

Mary's Call remains a very small family organization and is able to operate only through the assistance (time, talent, and donations) of friends. We hope that you will receive many blessings as a result of joining us in this ministry of prayer.

TABLE OF CONTENTS

4

A POWERFUL PRAYER TO BE SAID BEFORE PRAYING

"Almighty Father, I place the Precious Blood of Jesus before my lips before I pray, that my prayers may be purified before they ascend to Your divine altar."

-- St. Mary Magdalen de Pazzi

O JESUS

In union with your most precious blood poured out on the cross and offered in every mass, I offer you today my prayers, works, joys, sorrows and sufferings for the praise of Your holy name and all the desires of Your sacred heart; in reparation for sin, for the conversion of sinners, the union of all Christians and our final union with you in heaven.

8

"And I saw the River over which every soul must pass to reach the Kingdom of Heaven, and the name of the River was *SUFFERING*...and I saw the Boat which carries souls across the River, and the name of that Boat was... *LOVE*."

-- *St. John of the Cross*

I am calling you to **sincere prayer** with the heart so that every prayer of yours may be an encounter with God. In your work and in your everyday life, do put God in the first place.

Only by **prayer** can you understand and accept my messages and practice them in your life. Read Sacred Scripture, live it, and pray to understand the signs of the time. This is a special time. I am with you to draw you close to the Heart of my Son, Jesus. I want you to be children of the light and not of the darkness. Live what I am telling you. Thank you for having responded to my call.

Lord

Help me to remember that
nothing is impossible to prayer.

Because when I pray, I bring You close
and when You are close, I am not alone or
afraid. I call on You, and the world eases
around me.

There is comfort for my hurt ... and peace
from my worries. As one door closes,
I see another open wide before me.

So, let my whispered voice start each day
with the promise of prayer — certain that
with Your name on my lips ... and Your love
in my heart ... all things are ever possible.

*"Come to Me, all you who
labor and are heavy
burdened, and I will give you
rest..."*

11

GOD WANTS YOU

You have it in you to influence others and to accomplish far more than you have ever dreamed of accomplishing in the way of reflecting God's love to others.

But you can do this only if you bring out the best in yourself. You have the responsibility of continuing each day to grow and mature to the highest point that is possible for you to reach. God asks no more than that.

But He also asks no less than that. You may be reluctant, as Moses was, you may be inclined to say: "Lord, send someone else."

Your Lord wants you, and he will not be satisfied with anyone else but you, because you have the talents and the abilities that are suited to a particular task.

PRAYER FOR A FAMILY

O Dear Jesus,
I humbly implore You to grant Your special graces
to our family. May our home be the shrine of
peace, purity, love, labor and faith. I beg You, dear
Jesus, to protect and bless all of us, absent and
present, living and dead.

O Mary,
Loving Mother of Jesus, and our Mother, pray to
Jesus for our family, for all the families of the
world, to guard the cradle of the newborn, the
schools of the young and their vocations.

Blessed Saint Joseph,
Holy guardian of Jesus and Mary, assist us by
your prayers in all necessities of life. Ask of Jesus
that special grace which He granted to you to
watch over our home at the pillow of the sick and
dying, so that with Mary and with you, heaven may
find our family unbroken in the Sacred Heart of
Jesus. Amen.

PRAYER TO THE HOLY SPIRIT

Come, Holy Spirit, fill my heart with Your holy gifts.

Let my weakness be penetrated with Your strength this very day that I may fulfill all the duties of my state conscientiously, that I may do what is right and just.

Let my charity be such as to offend no one and hurt no one's feelings; so generous as to pardon sincerely any wrong done to me.

Assist me, O Holy Spirit, in all my trials of life, enlighten me in my ignorance, advise me in my doubts, strengthen me in my weakness, help me in all my needs, protect me in temptations and console me in afflictions.

Graciously hear me, O Holy Spirit, and pour Your light into my heart, my soul, and my mind.

Assist me to live a holy life and to grow in goodness and grace. Amen

IN TIME OF SUFFERING

A thought of Sister Faustina:

Oh, if only the suffering soul knew how much God loves it, it would die of joy and of an excess of happiness! One day, we shall know the value of suffering, but then we will no longer be able to suffer. The present moment is ours. (II, 304)

Jesus do not leave me alone in suffering. You know, Lord, how weak I am. I am an abyss of wretchedness, I am nothingness itself; So what will be so strange if You leave me alone and I fall? I am an infant, Lord, so I cannot get along by myself. However, beyond all abandonment I trust, and in spite of my own feeling I trust, and I am being completely transformed into trust — often in spite of what I feel. Do not lessen any of my sufferings, only give me the strength to bear them. Do with me as you please, Lord, only give me the grace to be able to love You in every event and circumstance. Lord, do not lessen my cup of bitterness, only give me the strength that I may be able to drink it all. Amen.

THE WEAVER

My life is but a weaving
Between my Lord and me;
I cannot choose the colors,
He worketh steadily.

Oft-times He weaveth sorrow,
And I, in foolish pride,
Forget He sees the upper,
And I the under side.

Not till the loom is silent
And the shuttles cease to fly,
Shall God unroll the canvas
And explain the reason why.

The dark threads are as needful,
In the Weaver's skillful hand,
As the threads of gold and silver
In the pattern He has planned.

He knows, He loves, He cares
Nothing this truth can dim;
He gives the very best to those,
Who leave the choice with Him.

NO TIME!

I knelt to pray ... but not for long,
I had too much to do.
Must hurry off and get to work,
For bills would soon come due.
And as I said a hurried prayer
Jumped up from off my knees,
My Christian duty now is done
My soul could be at ease.
All through the day I had no time
To speak a word of cheer.
No time to speak of Christ to friend,
They'd laugh at me, I feared.
No time — No time ... too much to do
That was my constant cry.
No time to give to those in need
At last ... t'was time to die.
And when before the Lord I came
I stood with downcast eyes.
Within His hand He held a book
It was the *Book of Life.*
He looked into the book and said,
"Your name I cannot find,
I once was going to write it down
But never found the time."

HEAVEN OPENED BY THE PRACTICE OF THE THREE HAIL MARYS

One of the greatest means of salvation is unquestionably the devotion to the Most Blessed Virgin. All the holy doctors of the church are unanimous in saying: "A devout servant of Mary shall never perish."

Regarding the devotion of the Three Hail Marys, our Lady revealed to St. Mechtilde:

18

"The first Hail Mary will be in honor of God the Father, whose omnipotence raised my soul so high above every other creature, that, after God, I have the greatest power in Heaven and on earth. In the hour of your death I will use that power of God the Father to keep any hostile power from you."

"The second Hail Mary will be in honor of God the Son, who communicated His inscrutable wisdom to me ... In the hour of your death I will fill your soul with the light of that wisdom so that all the darkness of ignorance and error will be dispelled."

"The third Hail Mary will be in honor of God the Holy Ghost, who filled my soul with the sweetness of His love and tenderness and mercy. In your last hour I will then change the bitterness of death into divine sweetness and delight."

Can there be an easier or a more acceptable practice for all than the recitation each day of three Hail Marys?

PRAYER IN TIME OF SICKNESS

O Jesus, You suffered and died for us;
You understand suffering;
Teach me to understand my suffering as You do;
To bear it in union with You;
To offer it with You to atone for my sins
And to bring Your grace to souls in need.
Calm my fears; increase my trust.
May I gladly accept Your holy will
And become more like You in trial.
If it be Your will, restore me to health so
that I may work for Your honor and glory
and the salvation of all men. Amen.

Mary, helper of the sick, pray for me.

PRAYER FOR HOSPITALIZATION

Jesus, I give You all those parts of my body which have suffered from illness. You know what it is like to endure pain. Let me see how You reshape and make that part of my body new, just as You and Your Father fashioned me with such exacting precious precision at the moment of my conception.

Give Your gift of wisdom to my Physician that He may be guided by the Holy Spirit in all He does.

Bless, too, my medication and my nurses so that their hands will become Your hands as they touch me.

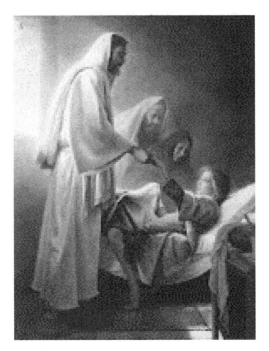

THE DIFFERENCE

I got up one morning and rushed
right into the day;
I had so much to accomplish that
I didn't have time to pray.
Problems just tumbled about me, and
heavier came each task.
"Why doesn't God help me?" I wondered.
He answered, "You didn't ask."
I wanted to see joy and beauty, but
the day toiled on, gray and bleak;
I wondered why God didn't show me.
He said, "But you didn't seek."
I tried to come into God's presence;
I used all my keys at the lock.
God gently and lovingly chided,
"My child, you didn't knock."
I woke up early this morning, and paused
before entering the day;
I had so much to accomplish that
I had to take time to pray.

PRAYER TO ST. JOSEPH

Over 1900 years old

Oh St. Joseph

Whose protection is so great, so strong, so prompt before the Throne of God, I place in you all my interests and desires. Oh St. Joseph do assist me by your powerful intercession and obtain for me from your Divine Son all spiritual blessings through Jesus Christ, Our Lord; so that having engaged here below your Heavenly power I may offer my Thanksgiving and Homage to the Loving Fathers. O St. Joseph, I never weary contemplating you and Jesus asleep in your arms. I dare not approach while He reposes near your heart. Press him in my name and kiss His fine Head for me and ask Him to return the Kiss when I draw my dying breath. St. Joseph, Patron of departing souls, pray for us. Amen.

THANKSGIVING

I asked God for strength,
that I might achieve ...
I was made weak,
that I might learn humbly to obey.
I asked for health,
that I might do greater things...
I was given infirmity,
that I might do better things...
I asked for riches,
that I might be happy...
I was given poverty,
that I might be wise.
I asked for power,
that I might have the praise of men...
I was given weakness,
that I might feel the need of God.
I asked for all things,
that I might enjoy life...
I was given life,
that I might enjoy all things.
I got nothing that I asked for,
but everything I had hoped for.
Almost despite myself,
my unspoken prayers were answered.
I am among all mankind, most richly blessed!

A PRAYER TO REDEEM LOST TIME

by St. Teresa of Avila

O my God! Source of all mercy! I acknowledge Your sovereign power. While recalling the wasted years that are past, I believe that You, Lord, can in an instant turn this loss to gain. Miserable as I am, yet I firmly believe that You can do all things.

Please restore to me the time lost, giving me Your grace, both now and in the future, that I may appear before You in "wedding garments." Amen

It is better to say one Our Father fervently and devoutly than a thousand with no devotion and full of distraction.

-- St. Edmund

MOST HUMBLE OF US ALL

In trying to know you, Mother, I came to know your Son.

In trying to seek you, Mother, I only found your Son.

In trying to touch you, Mother, I finally felt your Son.

In trying to hear you, Mother, the words were from your Son.

In trying to make you happy, the joy flowed from your Son.

In trying to love you, Mary, I have come to love your Son.

Most beautiful of Mothers, you are the humble one, for when we try to reach you, we end up with your Son.

Why can't we find you, Mother, you must be there with Him. But it's Jesus that we always find, in our world growing dim.

Your place above the angels, yet humblest of us all.

You always show us Jesus, no matter how we call.

Most humble of all mothers, your work is finally done.

Thank you blessed Mary, you have given us your Son.

IT'S UP TO YOU

Have YOU made someone happy, or made someone sad?

What have You done with the day that YOU had?

God gave it to You to do just as You would,

Did You do what was wicked or do what was good?

Did You hand out a smile or give 'em a frown?

Did You lift someone up, or push someone down?

Did You lighten some load, or some progress impede?

Did You look for a rose, or just gather a weed?

What did You do with your beautiful day?

God gave it to You, did you throw it away?

ALWAYS IN HIS CARE

When you're all alone and feel so lost, too weak to bear Life's heavy cross,

When the night is dark and there's no moon, or stars to brighten up the gloom...

When cares and troubles get you down. no friend or loved one is around,

When life seems just too hard to bear without someone who loves and cares...

Beyond the gloom of darkest night there is an Ever Shining Light,

That can't be seen by human eye but comes from God to you and I...

To let us know we're not alone, That beaming from our heavenly home

God's love is ever present there and we are always in His care.

-- Elizabeth B. Delea

God exists — Have You Found Him

28

A PRAYER FOR THOSE WHO LIVE ALONE

I live alone, dear Lord,
Stay by my side,
In all my daily needs,
Be Thou my guide.

Grant me good health,
For that indeed, I pray,
To carry on my work
From day to day.

Keep pure my mind,
My thoughts, my every deed.
Let me be kind, unselfish
In my neighbor's need.

Spare me from fire, from flood
Malicious tongues,
From thieves, from fear,
And evil ones.

If sickness or an accident befall,
Then humbly, Lord, I pray,
Hear, Thou my call,
And when I'm feeling low,
Or in despair,
Lift up my heart
And help me in my prayer.

I live alone, dear Lord,
Yet have no fear.
Because I feel Your Presence
Ever near.
Amen.

YOU NEED TO PRAY!

Because we do not see the value of prayer, we say we have no time for prayer.

FIRST, we need to pray, because our salvation depends on it.

St. Alphonsus Ligouri said: "If I had only one sermon to preach, I'd preach it on prayer." "For," he said, "if you pray, you will be saved; if you do not pray you will be lost."

Someone put it this way in rhyme:

> If you pray well, you'll live well.
> If you live well, you'll die well.
> If you die well, you won't go to hell.
> And if you don't go to hell, then all is well.

The plight of the world today and the victories of Satan in the world can be attributed to the single fact that we are relying too much on our own resources — ourselves, our sciences, our technologies — and not at all on prayer.

"We have been the recipients of the choicest bounties of heaven; we have been preserved these many years in peace and prosperity; we have grown in numbers, wealth, and power as no other nation has ever grown.

But we have forgotten God. We have forgotten the gracious hand which preserved us in peace and multiplied and enriched and strengthened us, and we have vainly imagined, in the deceitfulness of our hearts, that all these things were produced by some superior wisdom and virtue of our own.

Intoxicated with unbroken success, we have become too self-sufficient to feel the necessity of redeeming and preserving grace, too proud to pray to the God that made us."

-- Abraham Lincoln

THE UNIVERSAL PRAYER

Lord, I believe in you: increase my faith.
I trust in you: strengthen my trust.
I love you: let me love you more and more.
I am sorry for my sins: deepen my sorrow.

I worship you as my first beginning.
I long for you as my last end,
I praise you as my constant helper,
    and call on you as my loving protector.

Guide me by your wisdom,
    correct me with your justice,
    comfort me with your mercy,
    protect me with your power.

I offer you, Lord,
    my thoughts: to be fixed on you;
    my words: to have you for their theme;
    my actions: to reflect my love for you;

my sufferings: to be endured for your greater
glory.

I want to do what you ask of me:
in the way you ask,
for as long as you ask,
because you ask it.

Lord, enlighten my understanding,
strengthen my will,
purify my heart
and make me holy.

Help me to repent of my past sins
and to resist temptation in the future.

Help me to rise above my human weak-nesses
and to grow stronger as a Christian.

Let me love you, my Lord and my God,
and see myself as I really am:
a pilgrim in this world,
a Christian called to respect
and love all those whose lives I touch,
those in authority over me
and those under my authority,
my friends and my enemies.

Help me to conquer anger with gentleness,
greed by generosity, apathy by fervor.

Help me to forget myself
and reach out to others.

Make me prudent in planning,
courageous in taking risk,
patient in suffering,
unassuming in **prosperity**.

Keep me, Lord, **attentive** at prayer,
temperate in food and drink,
diligent in my work,
and firm in my intentions.

Let my conscience be clear,
my conduct without fault,
my speech blameless,
my life well-ordered.

Put me on guard
against my human weaknesses.

Let me cherish your love for me,
keep your law,
and come at last to your salvation.

Teach me to be aware
that this world is passing,
that my true future is the happiness of heaven,
that life on earth is short,
and the life to come eternal.

Help me to prepare for death
with a proper fear of judgment,
but a greater trust in your goodness.

Lead me safely through death
to the endless joy of heaven.

Grant this through Christ our Lord.
Amen.

*The more we pray, the more we
wish to pray.*
-- St. John Vianney

YOUR DAY

"Is anybody happier because you passed this way?

Does anyone remember that you spoke to them today?

The day is almost over, and its toiling time is through:

Is there anyone to utter now a kindly word of you?

Can you say tonight in parting with the day that's slipping past,

That you helped a single person of the many that you passed?

Is a single heart rejoicing over what you did or said?

Does the one whose hopes were fading now with courage look ahead?

Did you waste the day or use it? Was it well or sorely spent?

Did you leave a trail of kindness, or a scar of discontent?

As you close your eyes in slumber, do you think that God will say:

'You have earned one more tomorrow by what you did today'?"

--Author Unknown

TO OUR SAVIOUR

A Prayer by Saint Augustine

Sweet Jesus, let me know myself and let me know
Thee,
And desire nothing but Thee alone.
Sweet Jesus, let me hate myself and love Thee.
Let me do everything for the sake of Thee.

Sweet Jesus, let me humble myself and exalt
Thee,
And let me think of nothing but Thee alone.
Let me die to myself and live in Thee.
Let me take whatever happens as coming from
Thee.

Sweet Jesus, let me forsake myself and walk after
Thee.
And ever desire to follow Thee.
Let me fly from myself and take refuge in Thee,
That I may deserve to be defended by Thee.

Let me fear for myself and let me fear Thee,
And let me be among those chosen by Thee.
Let me distrust myself and put my trust in Thee.
Let me ever obey for the love of Thee.

Sweet Jesus, let me cling to nothing but only
Thee,
And let me be poor for the sake of Thee.
Sweet Jesus, look upon me that I may love Thee.
Call me that I may see Thee and forever possess
Thee.

A PRAYER TO THE BLESSED VIRGIN

O Most beautiful Flower of Mount Carmel, Fruitful Vine, Splendor of Heaven, Blessed Mother of the Son of God, Immaculate Virgin, assist me in this my necessity. O Star of the Sea, help me and show me You are my Mother.

O Holy Mary, Mother of God, Queen of Heaven and Earth, I humbly beseech You from the bottom of my heart, to succor me in this necessity; there are none that can withstand Your power. O, show me You are my Mother.

O Mary, conceived without sin, pray for us who have recourse to Thee. (3 times)

Sweet Mother, I place this cause in Your hands. (3 times)

POWER OF THE ROSARY

A THINKING PRAYER

To Father Gobbi, on October 7, 1983, Our Lady said:

Beloved sons, in the battle in which you are daily engaged against Satan and his crafty and dangerous seductions, and against the mighty armies of evil, apart from the special help given you by the angels of the Lord, it is necessary for you to employ a weapon which is both secure and invincible. This weapon is your prayer.

The prayer of my preference is the holy rosary. For this reason, in my apparitions I always ask that it be recited...

Father Gobbi, founder of "Marian Movement of Priests" said Our Lady told him through a locution that "who- ever prays a five-decade Rosary daily, every member of their family will be saved!"

WHY THE DAILY ROSARY?

· Pope John Paul II prayed the rosary every day.

· Our Lady has 48 titles. She selected this title at Fatima: "I am the Lady of the Rosary".

· St. Francis de Sales said the greatest method of praying is — Pray the Rosary.

· St. Thomas Aquinas preached for 40 straight days in Rome Italy on just the Hail Mary.

· St. John Vianney, patron of priests, was seldom seen without a rosary in his hand.

· The rosary is the scourge of the devil — Pope Adrian VI.

· The rosary is a treasure of graces — Pope Paul V.

· Padre Pio, the stigmatic priest said, "The rosary is THE WEAPON."

· Pope Leo XIII wrote nine encyclicals on the rosary.

· Pope John XXIII spoke 38 times about our Lady and the Rosary. He prayed 15 decades daily.

· St. Louis Marie Grignion de Monfort wrote: "The rosary is the most powerful weapon to touch the Heart of Jesus, Our Redeemer, who so loves His Mother."

· If you wish to obtain a favor — Pray the "54-day ROSARY NOVENA."

THE FIFTEEN PROMISES OF MARY TO CHRISTIANS WHO RECITE THE ROSARY

1. Whoever shall faithfully serve me by the recitation of the rosary, shall receive signal graces.

2. I promise my special protection and the greatest graces to all those who shall recite the rosary.

3. The rosary shall be a powerful armor against hell, it will destroy vice, decrease sin, and defeat heresies.

4. It will cause virtue and good works to flourish; it will obtain for souls the abundant mercy of God; it will withdraw the hearts of men from the love of the world and its vanities and will lift them to the desire of eternal things. Oh, that souls would sanctify themselves by this means.

5. The soul which recommends itself to me by the recitation of the rosary shall not perish.

6. Whoever shall recite the rosary devoutly, applying himself to the consideration of its sacred mysteries shall never be conquered by misfortune. God will not chastise him in His justice, he shall not perish by an unprovided death; if he be just, he shall remain in the grace of God, and become worthy of eternal life.

7. Whoever shall have a true devotion for the rosary shall not die without the sacraments of

the Church.

8. Those who are faithful to recite the rosary shall have during their life and at their death the light of God and the plenitude of His graces; at the moment of death they shall participate in the merits of the saints in paradise.

9. I shall deliver from purgatory those who have been devoted to the rosary.

10. The faithful children of the rosary shall merit a high degree of glory in heaven.

11. You shall obtain all you ask of me by the recitation of the rosary.

12. All those who propagate the holy rosary shall be aided by me in all their necessities.

13. I have obtained from my Divine Son that all the advocates of the rosary shall have for intercessors the entire celestial court during their life and at the hour of their death.

14. All who recite the rosary are my sons, and brothers of my only son, Jesus Christ.

15. Devotions of my rosary is a great sign of predestination.

HOW TO SAY THE ROSARY

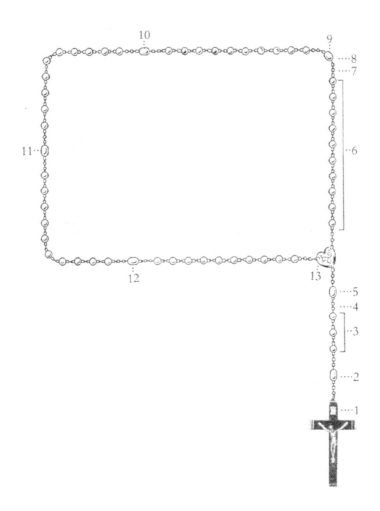

1. Make the Sign of the Cross and say The Apostles' Creed.

2. Say *Our Fathers.*

3. Say 3 *Hail Marys.*

4. Say the *Glory Be to the Father.*

5. Announce the First Mystery; then say the *Our Father.*

6. Say 10 *Hail Marys*

7. Say the *Glory Be to the Father*

8. Say the *O My Jesus*

9. Announce the Second Mystery; then say the *Our Father;* 10 *Hail Marys, Glory Be* and *O My Jesus.*

10. Announce the Third Mystery; then say the *Our Father;* 10 *Hail Marys, Glory Be* and *O My Jesus.*

11. Announce the Fourth Mystery; then say the *Our Father;* 10 *Hail Marys, Glory Be* and *O My Jesus.*

12. Announce the Fifth Mystery; then say the *Our Father;* 10 *Hail Marys, Glory Be* and *O My Jesus.*

13. Conclude by saying the *Hail, Holy Queen.*

THE APOSTLES' CREED

I believe in God, the Father Almighty, Creator of heaven and earth; and in Jesus Christ, His only Son, our Lord; who was conceived by the Holy Ghost, born of the Virgin Mary, suffered under Pontius Pilate, was crucified, died, and was buried. He descended into Hell; the third day He arose again from the dead; He ascended into Heaven, sitteth at the right hand of God, the Father Almighty; from thence He shall come to judge the living and the dead. *I believe in the Holy Ghost, the Holy Catholic Church, the Communion of Saints, the forgiveness of sins, the resurrection of the body, and life everlasting. Amen.

OUR FATHER

Our Father, Who art in Heaven, hallowed be Thy Name. Thy kingdom come, Thy will be done on earth as it is in Heaven. *Give us this day our daily bread, and forgive us our trespasses, as we forgive those who trespass against us. And lead us not into temptation but deliver us from evil. Amen.

HAIL MARY

Hail Mary, full of grace, the Lord is with thee; blessed art thou among women, and blessed is the Fruit of thy womb, Jesus. *Holy Mary, Mother of God, pray for us sinners, now and at the hour of our death. Amen.

GLORY BE

Glory be to the Father, and to the Son, and to the Holy Ghost. *As it was in the beginning, is now, and ever shall be, world without end. Amen.

O MY JESUS

To be said after the Glory Be to the Father following each decade of the Rosary. All pray it together.

O my Jesus, forgive us our sins, save us from the fires of Hell, lead all souls to Heaven, especially those who are in most need of Thy mercy.

HAIL, HOLY QUEEN

Hail, holy Queen, Mother of mercy, our life, our sweet- ness and our hope. To thee do we cry, poor banished children of Eve. To thee do we send up our sighs, mourning and weeping in this valley of tears. Turn then, most gracious advocate, thine eyes of mercy towards us. And after this our exile, show unto us the blessed Fruit of thy womb, Jesus. O clement, O loving, O sweet Virgin Mary.

V. Pray for us, O holy Mother of God.

R. That we made be made worthy of the promises of Christ.

Note: When the Rosary is said aloud by two or more persons, one person is the leader; he says the first part of each prayer, and everyone else answers by saying the remainder of the prayer (designated hereby an asterisk). The O My Jesus and the body of the Hail, Holy Queen are said by all together.

THE MYSTERIES OF THE ROSARY THE JOYFUL MYSTERIES

THE ANNUNCIATION

"Do not be afraid, Mary, for you have found favor with God. And behold, you will conceive in your womb and bear a Son, and you shall call His name Jesus."

Luke 1:30-31

THE VISITATION

"Blessed are you among women, and blessed is the fruit of your womb! And why is this granted to me, that the mother of my Lord should come to me?"

Luke: 1:42-23

THE NATIVITY

Mary gave birth to her first-born Son and wrapped Him in swaddling clothes, and laid Him in a manger, because there was no room for them in the inn.

Luke 2:7

THE PRESENTATION

When the day came to purify him according to the law of Moses, the couple brought him up to Jerusalem so that he could be presented to the Lord, for it is written in the law of the Lord, "Every first-born male shall be consecrated to the Lord."

Luke 2:22-23

THE FINDING IN THE TEMPLE

On the third day they came upon him in the temple sitting in the midst of the teachers, listening to them and asking them questions.

Luke 2:46

THE SORROWFUL MYSTERIES

THE AGONY IN THE GARDEN

Jesus prayed: "Abba, Father, all things are possible to You; remove this cup from Me; yet not what I will, but what You will."

Mark 14:36

THE SCOURGING

Pilate, wishing to satisfy the crowd, released for

them Barabbas; and having scourged Jesus, he
delivered Him to be crucified.

Mark 15:15

THE CROWNING WITH THORNS

The soldiers clothed Him in a purple cloak, and
placing a crown of thorns they put it on Him. And
they began to salute Him, "Hail, King of the Jews!"

Mark 15: 17-18

THE CARRYING OF THE CROSS

They took Jesus, and He went out, bearing His
own cross, to the place called the place of the
skull, which is called in Hebrew Golgotha.

John 19:17

THE CRUCIFIXION

Jesus, crying with a loud voice, said, "Father, into
Your hands I commit My spirit!" And having said
this He breathed His last.

Luke 23:46

THE GLORIOUS MYSTERIES

THE RESURRECTION

"Do not be afraid; for I know that you seek Jesus who was crucified. He is not here, for He has risen, as He said."

Matthew 28:5-6

THE ASCENSION

As the Apostles looked on, Jesus was lifted up, and a cloud took Him out of their sight ... "This Jesus, who was taken from you into heaven, will come in the same way as you saw Him go into heaven."

Acts 1:9,11

THE DESCENT OF THE HOLY GHOST

All were filled with the Holy Spirit. They began to express themselves in foreign tongues and make bold proclamation as the Spirit prompted them.

Acts 2:2,4

THE ASSUMPTION

A great sign appeared in the sky, a woman clothed with the sun, with the moon under her feet, and on her head a crown of twelve stars.

Revelations 12:1

THE CORONATION

You are the glory of Jerusalem ... you are the splendid boast of our people ... God is pleased with what you have wrought. May you be blessed by the Lord Almighty forever and ever.

Judith 15: 9-10

MYSTERIES OF LIGHT

THE BAPTISM OF JESUS

The heavens were opened and he saw the Spirit of God descending like a dove. And a voice came from heaven "This is my beloved Son, with whom I am well pleased."

Matthew 3:16-17

WEDDING AT CANA

When the wine ran short, the mother of Jesus said

to Him, "They have no wine." She said to the
servants, "Do whatever he tells you."

John 2:3,5

PROCLAMATION OF THE KINGDOM

Now after John was arrested, Jesus came into
Galilee, preaching the gospel of God and saying,
"The time is fulfilled, and the kingdom of God is at
hand; repent and believe in the gospel."

Mark 1:14-15

THE TRANSFIGURATION

He took with Him Peter and John and James, and
went up on the mountain to pray. And as he was
praying, the appearance of His face altered and
His clothing became dazzling white.

Luke 9:28-29

INSTITUTION OF THE EUCHARIST

Now, as they were eating, Jesus took bread, and
blessed, and broke it, and gave it to the disciples
and said, "Take, eat; this is my body."

Matthew 26:26

TO OUR LADY

Lovely Lady dressed in Blue,
Teach me how to pray!
God was just your little Boy,
Tell me what to say!
Did you lift Him up, sometimes,
Gently on your knee?
Did you sing to Him the way
Mother does to me?
Did you hold His hand at night?
Did you ever try
Telling stories of the world?
O! And did He cry?
Do you really think He cares
If I tell Him things —
Little things that happen?
And
Do the Angels' wings
Make a noise? And can He hear
Me if I speak low?
Does He understand me now?
Tell me — for you know?
Lovely Lady dressed in blue,
Teach me how to pray!
God was just your little Boy.
And you know the way.

CONSECRATION OF THE FAMILY TO THE SACRED HEARTS OF JESUS AND MARY

Most Holy Hearts of Jesus and Mary, united in perfect love, as you look upon us with mercy and caring, we consecrate our hearts, our lives, our family to you.

We know the beautiful example of your home in Nazareth was meant to be a model for each of our families. We hope to have, with your help, the unity and strong, enduring love you gave to one another.

May our home be filled with joy. May sincere affection, patience, tolerance and mutual respect be freely given to all. May our prayers be filled with the needs of others, not just ourselves and may we always be close to your sacraments.

Bless those who are present, as well as those who are absent, both the living and the dead; may peace be among us and when we are tested, grant us the Christian acceptance of God's will.

Keep our family close to your Hearts, may your special protection be with us always.

Most Sacred Hearts of Jesus and Mary, hear our prayer.

LORD — I NEED YOU

O most good and loving Lord,
You know my weaknesses and my needs.
You know how many bad habits and vices I have.

You know how often I am burdened,
    tempted, shaken and stained by sin.
I come to You for healing.

I pray to You for comfort and support.
I speak to You, who know all things, to
    whom my inmost thoughts are evident.

You alone can adequately comfort me
    and help me.
You know what good things I need most,
    and You know how poor I am in virtue.

I stand before You, asking for your grace
    and imploring your mercy.
Feed me, for I am hungry.

Inflame my coldness with the fire of your love.
Illuminate my blindness with the light of your
    presence.

Turn my eyes from all that is not You
Turn all oppression into patience.
Make all that leads me from You not worth
    thinking about.

Make me forget it all.
Lift up my heart to You in heaven, and let me not
wander aimlessly about in this world.

YOUR CROSS

The Everlasting God has in His wisdom foreseen from eternity the cross that He now presents to you as a gift from His inmost Heart. This cross He now sends you He has considered with His all-knowing eyes, understood with His divine mind, tested with His wise justice, warmed with loving arms and weighed with His own hands to see that it be not one inch too large and not one ounce too heavy for you. He has blessed it with His holy Name, anointed it with His grace, perfumed it with His consolation, taken one last glance at you and your courage, and then sent it to you from heaven, a special greeting from God to you, an alms of the all-merciful love of God.

-- St. Francis de Sales

PASSING THROUGH

As I wander down life's winding path
    with chasms on each side,
I try to keep my eyes on God
    and with His Word abide.
I try to do the many things
    I know He wants me to,
for on this earth I've little time
    'cause I'm just passing through.
I know that every step I take
    requires His guiding hand,
for danger lurks at every turn
    that bears the devil's brand.
And by myself, I would be lost
    to seek without a clue,
The path to everlasting life
    while I am passing through.
I must remember everyday
    to quell my foolish pride,
For all my efforts, naught would be,
    without Him by my side.
Just like the pilgrim on life's road
    I've faith in Jesus,
Who will guide me in the wilderness
    while I am passing through.
So with bowed head, I ask my Lord,
    "Correct me when I stray
and give me strength to overcome
    temptations everyday."
Then when my life is finished
    and my deeds He does review,
I'll know I did my very best
    while I was passing through.

--Thomas C. Gallagher

MARY'S CHRISTMAS DREAM

I had a dream, Joseph. I don't understand it, not really, but I think it was about a birthday celebration for our Son. I think that was what it was all about. The people had been preparing for it for about six weeks. They had decorated the house and bought new clothes. They'd gone shopping many times and bought elaborate gifts. It was peculiar, though, because the presents weren't for our Son. They wrapped them in beautiful paper and tied them with lovely bows and stacked them under a tree. Yes, a tree, Joseph, right in their house. They'd decorated the tree also. The branches were full of glowing balls and sparkling ornaments. There was a figure on the top of the tree. It looked like an angel might look. Oh, it was beautiful. Everyone was laughing and happy. They were all excited about the gifts. They gave the gifts to each other, Joseph, not to our Son. I don't think they even knew Him. They never mentioned His name. Doesn't it seem odd for people to go to all that trouble to celebrate someone's birthday if they don't know Him. I had the strangest feeling that if our Son had gone to this celebration He would have been intruding. Everything was so beautiful, Joseph, and everyone so gay, but it made me want to cry. How sad for Jesus — not to be wanted at His own birthday party. I'm glad it was only a dream. How terrible, Joseph, if it had been real.

61

LISTEN TO ME

Just stop a while and listen to Me —
I have a question to ask of thee
Why are you ignoring my Mother?

I chose her to be my very own
And greater perfection was never known.
Why are you ignoring my Mother?

I was born through her so we all would be
Spiritual members of one family —
Why are you ignoring my Mother?

I've sent her to you with a message divine —
Not once or twice but many a time
And still you're ignoring my Mother!
Like a wreath of graces her Rosary she's given
To her loving children as a key to heaven —
And still you're ignoring my Mother!

She came with my message to La Salette
But those requests have not been met
Why are you ignoring my Mother?

I sent her again — to the cave at Lourdes
But just as before you spurned her words
Why are you ignoring my Mother?

To the fields of Fatima again she came —
For prayers and sacrifice in her Son's Name
and still you're ignoring my Mother?

I sent her to earth from heaven above —

So you would give her your honor and love
And still you're ignoring my Mother!

When you ignore my Mother you ignore her Son
Because to Me — she's the dearest one!
Why are you ignoring my Mother?

You'd better amend and do not tarry
The ideal way to Jesus — is Mary!
So stop ignoring my Mother!

*Must one wait for some misfortune
in order to look for God?*

LITANY OF THE HOLY NAME OF JESUS

Lord, have mercy on us.
Christ, have mercy on us.
Lord, have mercy on us.
Christ, hear us.

Christ, graciously hear us.
God the Father of heaven:
> *Have mercy on us.*
God the Son, Redeemer of the world:
God the Holy Spirit:

Holy Trinity, one God:
Jesus, Son of the Living God:
Jesus, splendor of the Father:
Jesus, brightness of eternal light:

Jesus, King of Glory:
Jesus, Son of Justice:
Jesus, Son of the Virgin Mary:
Jesus, most amiable:

Jesus, most admirable:
Jesus, mighty God:
Jesus, Father of the world to come:
Jesus, Angel of the great counsel:

Jesus, most powerful:
Jesus, most patient:
Jesus, most obedient:
Jesus, meek and humble of heart:

Jesus, lover of chastity:
Jesus, lover of us:
Jesus, God of Peace:
Jesus, Author of Life:

65

Jesus, model of virtues:
Jesus, zealous for souls:
Jesus, our God:
Jesus, our refuge:

Jesus, Father of the poor:
Jesus, treasure of the faithful:
Jesus, Good Shepherd:
Jesus, true Light:

Jesus, eternal wisdom:
Jesus, infinite goodness:
Jesus, our way and our life:
Jesus, joy of angels:

Jesus, King of Patriarchs:
Jesus, Master of the Apostles:
Jesus, teacher of the evangelists:
Jesus, strength of martyrs:

Jesus, light of confessors:
Jesus, purity of virgins:
Jesus, crown of all saints.
Be merciful: *Spare us, O Jesus.*

Be merciful: *Graciously hear us, O Jesus.*
From all evil: *Jesus deliver us.*
From all sin:
From thy wrath:

From the snares of the devil:
From the spirit of fornication:
From everlasting death:
From neglect of thy inspirations:

Through the mystery of thy Incarnation:
Through thy Nativity:
Through thy infancy:

66

Through thy most divine life:

Through thy labors:
Through thy agony and passion:
Through thy cross and dereliction:
Through thy weariness and faintness:

Through thy death and burial:
Through thy Resurrection:
Through thy Ascension:
Through thy joys:

Through thy glory:
Through thy institution of the Blessed
Sacrament. Lamb of God who takes away
the sins of the world:
Spare us, O Jesus.
Lamb of God, who takes away the sins of
the world:

Graciously hear us, O Jesus.
Lamb of God who takes away the sins of
the world:
Have mercy on us, O Jesus.
Jesus, hear us. *Jesus, graciously hear us.*

We will praise thee, O God.
And we will call upon thy name.

O Lord Jesus Christ, who has said, "Ask and you
shall receive, seek and you shall find; knock and it
shall be opened unto you," grant, we beseech
thee, that we may love thee with a whole heart, in
our words and in our work, and never cease, *to
praise thy name. Amen.*

PRAYER FOR A HAPPY DEATH

O Jesus, while adoring Your last breath, I pray You to receive mine. In the uncertainty whether I shall have the command of my senses when I shall depart out of this world, I offer You from this moment my agony and all the pains of my passing away. You are my Father and my Savior, and I give back my soul into Your hands. I desire that my last moment may be united to the moment of Your death, and that the last beat of my heart may be an act of pure love for You.
Amen

PEACE PRAYER

Lord, make me an instrument of Your peace. Where there is hatred, let me sow love.

Where there is injury, pardon. Where there is

doubt, faith. Where there is despair, hope. Where there is darkness, light. And where there is sadness, joy.

O Divine Master, grant that I may not so much seek to be consoled, as to console; to be understood, as to under- stand; to be loved, as to love. For it is in giving that we receive, it is in pardoning that we are pardoned, and it is in dying that we are born to Eternal Life!

-- St. Francis

68

THE LITANY OF THE BLESSED VIRGIN MARY

Lord have mercy on us.
Christ have mercy on us.
Lord, have mercy on us, Christ, hear us.
Christ, graciously hear us.

God the Father of Heaven,
Have mercy on us.
God the Son, Redeemer of the world,
Have mercy on us.

God the Holy Spirit,
Have mercy on us.
Holy Trinity, One God,
Have mercy on us.

Holy Mary, *(pray for us)*
Holy Mother of God,
Holy Virgin of virgins,
Mother of Christ,

Mother of divine grace,
Mother most pure,
Mother most chaste,
Mother inviolate,

Mother undefiled,
Mother most amiable,
Mother most admirable,
Mother of good counsel,

Mother of our Creator,
Mother of our Saviour,
Mother of the Church,
Virgin most prudent,

Virgin most venerable,
Virgin most renowned,
Virgin most powerful,
Virgin most merciful,

Virgin most faithful,
Mirror of justice,
Seat of wisdom,
Cause of our joy,

Spiritual vessel,
Vessel of honor,
Singular vessel of devotion,
Mystical rose,

Tower of David,
Tower of ivory,
House of gold,
Ark of the covenant,

Gate of Heaven,
Morning star,
Health of the sick,
Refuge of sinners,

Comforter of the afflicted,
Help of Christians,
Queen of angels,
Queen of patriarchs,

Queen of prophets,
Queen of apostles,
Queen of martyrs,
Queen of confessors,

Queen of virgins,
Queen of all saints,
Queen conceived without Original Sin,

Queen assumed into Heaven,

Queen of the most holy Rosary,
Queen of peace,
Lamb of God, Who takest away the sins of the world,

    Spare us, O Lord.

Lamb of God, Who takest away the sins of the world,

    Graciously hear us, O Lord.

Lamb of God Who takest away the sins of the world,

    Have mercy on us.

V. Pray for us, O Holy Mother of God.
R. That we may be made worthy of the promises of Christ.

LET US PRAY

Grant, we beseech You, O Lord God, that we Your servants may enjoy perpetual health of mind and body and by the glorious intercession of the Blessed Mary ever Virgin, be delivered from present sorrow and enjoy everlasting happiness. Through Christ Our Lord. Amen.

There is only one way to find God, and that is by prayer.

-- St. Teresa of Avila

PRAYER OF SELF-DEDICATION

Lord Jesus Christ, take all my freedom,

My memory, my understanding, and my will.

All that I have and cherish You have given me.

I surrender it all to be guided by Your will.

Your grace and Your love are wealth enough for me.

Give me these, Lord Jesus, and I ask for nothing more.

LITANY OF THE SACRED HEART OF JESUS

Lord, have mercy. — Lord, have mercy.
Christ, have mercy. — Christ have mercy.
Lord, have mercy. — Lord, have mercy.
Christ, hear us. — Christ, graciously hear us.

God the Father in heaven, — Have mercy on us.
God the Son, Redeemer of the world,
God the Holy Spirit,
Holy Trinity, one God,

Heart of Jesus, Son of the eternal Father,
Heart of Jesus, formed by the Holy Spirit in the
womb of the Virgin Mary,
Heart of Jesus, united with God's eternal Word,

Heart of Jesus, of limitless majesty.
Heart of Jesus, temple of God among us,
Heart of Jesus, shrine of the Most High,
Heart of Jesus, house of God and gate of heaven,

Heart of Jesus, glowing with love for us,
Heart of Jesus, overflowing with goodness and
love, Heart of Jesus, full of kindness and love,
Heart of Jesus, fountain of all holiness.

Heart of Jesus, worthy of all praise,
Heart of Jesus, king and center of all hearts,
Heart of Jesus, treasure-house of wisdom and
knowledge.
Heart of Jesus, tabernacle of God's fullness,

Heart of Jesus, in whom the Father is well-
pleased, Heart of Jesus, of whose fullness we
have all received,
Heart of Jesus, desire of the everlasting hills,

73

Heart of Jesus, patient and full of mercy,

Heart of Jesus, generous to all who turn to you,
Heart of Jesus, source of life and holiness,
Heart of Jesus, atonement for our sins,
Heart of Jesus, overwhelmed with reproaches,

Heart of Jesus, bruised for our sins,
Heart of Jesus, obedient all the way to death,
Heart of Jesus, pierced with a lance,
Heart of Jesus, source of all consolation,

Heart of Jesus, our life and resurrection,
Heart of Jesus, our peace and reconciliation,
Heart of Jesus, sacrifice for sin,
Heart of Jesus, salvation of all who trust in you,

Heart of Jesus, hope of all who die in you,
Heart of Jesus, delight of all the saints,
Lamb of God, you take away all the sins
of the world, — *Spare us, O Lord.*

Lamb of God, you take away the sins
of the world, — *Graciously hear us, O Lord.*
Lamb of God, you take away the sins of
the world, — *Have mercy on us.*

Jesus, gentle and humble of heart,

—*Touch our hearts and make them like your own.*

Let us pray.

Father, we rejoice in the gifts of love we have
received from the heart of Jesus your Son.

Open our hearts to share his life and continue to
bless us with his love.

We ask this through our Lord Jesus Christ your son, who lives and reigns with you and the Holy Spirit, one God, forever and ever.

Amen.

LITANY OF ST. JOSEPH

Lord, have mercy. — *Lord, have mercy.*
Christ, have mercy. — *Christ, have mercy.*
Lord, have mercy. — *Lord, have mercy.*

Christ, hear us.
   —*Christ, graciously hear us.*
God the Father in heaven,
   — *Have mercy on us.*

God the Son, Redeemer of the world,
God the Holy Spirit,
Holy Trinity, one God,
St. Joseph — *Pray for us.*

Renowned scion of David,
Light of patriarchs,
Husband of the Mother of God,
Chaste guardian of the Virgin,

Foster-father of the Son of God,
Watchful defender of Christ,
Head of the holy family,
Joseph, most just,

Joseph, most pure,
Joseph, most prudent,
Joseph, most valiant,
Joseph, most obedient,

Joseph, most faithful,
Mirror of patience,
Lover of poverty,
Model of artisans,
Glory of domestic life,

Guardian of virgins,
Consolation of those in trouble,

76

Hope of the sick,
Patron of the dying,
Terror of demons,

Protector of holy Church.
Lamb of God, you take away the sins of the world,
— *Spare us, O Lord.*
Lamb of God, you take away the sins of the world,
— *Graciously hear us, O Lord.*

Lamb of God, you take away the sins of the world,
— *Have mercy on us.*
He made him lord of his household,
— *And ruler over all his possessions.*

Let us pray.
God, in your infinite wisdom and love you chose
Joseph to be the husband of Mary, the mother of
your Son. May we have the help of his prayers in
heaven and enjoy his protection on earth. We ask
this through Christ our Lord. Amen

THREE VERY BEAUTIFUL PRAYERS

Which are very useful to a dying person and should be prayed often as an act of mercy.

There once was a Pope in Rome who was surrounded by many sins. The Lord God struck him with a fatal illness. When he saw that he was dying he summoned Cardinals, Bishops and learned persons and said to them: "My dear friends! What comfort can you give me now that I must die, and when I deserve eternal damnation for my sins?" No one answered him. One of them, a pious curate named John, said: "Father, why do you doubt the Mercy of God?" The Pope replied: "What comfort can you give me now that I must die and fear that I'll be damned for my sins?" John replied: "I'll read three prayers over you; I hope you'll be comforted and that you'll obtain mercy from God." The Pope was unable to say more. The curate and all those present knelt and said an Our Father, then the following Prayers:

FIRST PRAYER

Lord Jesus Christ! Thou Son of God and Son of the Virgin Mary, God and Man, You who in fear sweated blood for us on the Mount of Olives in order to bring peace, and to offer Thy Most Holy Death to God Thy Heavenly Father for the salvation of this dying person ... If it be, however, that by his sins he merits eternal damnation, then may it be deflected from him. This, Oh Eternal

78

Father through Our Lord Jesus Christ, Thy Dear
Son, Who liveth and reigneth in union with the
Holy Spirit now and forever. Amen.

SECONDPRAYER

Lord Jesus Christ! You Who meekly died on the
trunk of the Cross for us, submitting Thy Will
completely to Thy Heavenly Father in order to
bring peace and to offer Thy most Holy Death to
Thy Heavenly Father in order to free ... (this
person) ... and to hide from him what he has
earned with his sins; grant this O Eternal Father!
Through Our Lord Jesus Thy Son, Who liveth and
reigneth with Thee in union with the Holy Spirit
now and forever. Amen.

THIRD PRAYER

Lord Jesus Christ! Thou who remained silent to
speak through the mouths of the Prophets: I have
drawn Thee to me through Eternal Love, which
Love drew Thee from Heaven into the body of the
Virgin, which Love drew Thee from the body of the
Virgin into the valley of this needful world, which
Love kept Thee 33 years in this world, and as a
sign of Great Love, Thou hast given Thy Holy
Body as True Food and Thy Holy Blood as True
Drink, as a sign of Great Love, Thou has
consented to be a prisoner and to be led from one
judge to another and as a sign of Great Love Thou

has consented to be condemned to death, and hast consented to die and to be buried and truly risen, and appeared to Thy Holy Mother and all the Holy Apostles, and as a sign of Great Love Thou hast ascended, under Thy own Strength and Power, and sitteth at the Right Hand of God thy Heavenly Father, and Thou has sent Thy Holy Spirit into the hearts of Thy Apostles and the hearts of all who hope and believe in Thee through Thy Sign of Eternal Love, open Heaven today and take this dying person ... and all his sins into the Realm of Thy Heavenly Father, that he may reign with Thee now and forever. Amen.

Meanwhile the Pope died. The curate persevered to the third hour, then the Pope appeared to him in body and comforting him; his countenance as brilliant as sun, his clothes as white as snow, and he said: "My dear brother! Whereas I was supposed to be a child of damnation I've become a child of happiness. As you recited the first Prayer many of my sins fell from me as rain from Heaven, and as you recited the second Prayer I was purified, as a goldsmith purifies gold in a hot fire. I was still further purified as you recited the third Prayer. Then I saw Heaven open and the Lord Jesus standing on the right Hand of God the Father Who said to me: "Come, all thy sins are forgiven thee, you'll be and remain in the Realm of My Father forever. Amen!"

With these words my soul separated from my body and the Angels of God led it to Eternal Joy.

As the curate heard this he said: *"Oh Holy Father! I can't tell these things to anyone, for they won't believe me."*

Then the Pope said: *"Truly I tell thee, the Angel of God stands with me and has written the prayers in letters of gold for the consolement of all sinners. If a person had committed all the sins in the world, but that the three Prayers shall have been read (over Him) at his end (death), all his sins will be forgiven him, even though his soul was supposed to suffer until the Last Judgement, it will be redeemed (freed)"*

"The person who hears them read, he won't die an unhappy death, also in whose house they will be read. Therefore take these prayers and carry them into St. Peter's Basilica and lay them in the Chapel named the Assumption of Mary, for certain consolation. The person who will be near death, who reads them or hears them read gains 400 years indulgence for the days he was supposed to suffer in Purgatory because of his guilt. Also who reads this Prayer or hears it read, the hour of his death shall be revealed to him." Amen!

FATHER, WE THANK THEE

Father, we thank Thee:
For peace within our favored land,
For plenty from Thy bounteous hand,
For means to give to those in need,
For grace to help in thought and deed,
For faith to walk, our hands in Thine,
For truth to know Thy law divine,
For strength to work with voice and pen,
For love to serve our fellow men,
For light the goal ahead to see,
For life to use alone for Thee,
Father, we thank Thee.

--Grenville Kleiser

PRODIGAL

This earth has been my home so long,
And I have loved it well,
But one day I must leave it,
Just when I cannot tell.

The hour and the minute
I am scheduled to depart,
Was long ago decided,
And is written on God's heart.

This is a great old world, and how
I wish that I could stay,
But the years keep going faster,
And the hours slip away.

But as I near the turning
Of the road, I pause to view
The yesterdays I've left behind Me,
as I journey through

One year into another,
'Til they form a silver chain,
There are things I would do over,
Some I would not do again.

Though "Old sins cast long shadows,"
However long confessed,
With all my heart I do believe
I'll find a place to rest

Within the arms of Jesus,
Where no heartache and no pain,
Will ever be allowed to touch
This prodigal again.
And throughout all eternity,
My greatest joy will be,

That the Shepherd left His ninety-nine,
...To come in search of me!

--Grace E. Easley

Divine heart of Jesus
In Thee I trust
Trust him when the dark clouds assail thee,
Trust him when thy strength is small,

Trust Him
When to simply trust Him,
Seems the hardest thing of all.
Trust Him, He is ever faithful;

Trust Him, for His will is best,
Trust Him, for the heart of Jesus
Is the only place of rest.

Trust Him then through doubts and sunshine;
All thy cares upon Him cast,
Till the storms of life are over,
And Thy trusting days are past.

PRAYER FOR A PEACEFUL SPIRIT

Slow me down, Lord.
Ease my pounding heart,
Quiet my racing mind,
Steady my hurried steps.

Admidst the confusion of my days
Give me the calmness of the everlasting hills. Help
me to know the magical
Restoring power of sleep.

Teach me the art of taking time off
Of slowing down to look at a flower,
To chat with a friend,
To read a few lines from a good book.

Remind me each day
That there is more to life
Than increasing its speed.

Let me look upwards
Into the branches of a towering oak,
And know that it grew great and strong
Because it grew slowly and well.

Slow me down, Lord.
Teach me to be gentle and humble of heart,
So that I may find rest for my soul.

PRAYER IN TIME OF LOSS

Lord Jesus, someone whom I love very much has died and there is an empty space I cannot fill.

My heart aches and inside I feel so stiff and tired. Help me, dear Jesus, to look straight at that empty space and not be frightened.

Help me to be glad for him/her because he/she is happy with you.

And, oh dear Lord, help me to be unafraid to walk this earth without him/her, but to take my strength and comfort from your LOVE.

A PRAYER FOR THE FORGOTTEN DEAD

O merciful God, take pity on those souls who have no particular friends and intercessors to recommend them to You, who either through negligence of those who are alive or through length of time, are forgotten by all. Spare them, O Lord, and remember Your own when others forget to appeal to Your mercy. Let not the souls You have created be parted from You, their Creator.

CONSECRATING THE LAST TWO HOURS OF OUR LIFE TO THE MOST HOLY VIRGIN

by Rev. Fr. Idlefonso M. Izaguirre, O.P.

Prostrated at thy feet, and humiliated by my sins, but full of confidence in thee, O Mary! I beg thee to accept the petition my heart is going to make. It is for my last moments, Dear Mother I wish to request thy protection and maternal love so that in the decisive instant thou wilt do all thy love can suggest in my behalf.

To thee, O Mother of my soul, I consecrate **THE LAST TWO HOURS** of my life. Come to my side to receive my last breath and when death has cut the thread of my days, tell Jesus, presenting to Him my soul, "**I LOVE IT**". That word alone will be enough to procure for me the benediction of my God and the happiness of seeing thee for all eternity.

I put my trust in thee, my Mother and hope it will not be in vain.

O Mary! Pray for thy child and lead him to Jesus. Amen.

"Abandoning the Mother is but one step from abandoning the Son."

PRAYER BEFORE A CRUCIFIX

Look down upon me good and gentle Jesus, while before Thy face I humbly kneel and with burning soul pray and beseech Thee to fix deep in my heart lively sentiments of faith, hope and charity, true contrition for my sins and a firm purpose of amendment, while I contemplate with great love and tender pity The Five Wounds, pondering over them within me and calling to mind the words which David Thy prophet said of Thee my Jesus, "They have pierced My Hands and My Feet, they have numbered all My Bones." (Ps. 21, 17-18)

Our Father, Hail Mary, Glory Be, for Holy Father's intentions

ANIMA CHRIST!

Soul of Christ, sanctify me.
Body of Christ, save me.
Blood of Christ, inebriate me.
Water from the side of Christ, wash me.
Passion of Christ, strengthen me.
O good Jesus, hear me.
Within Thy wounds hide me.
Suffer me not to be separated from Thee.
From the malignant enemy, defend me.
In the hour of my death, call me.
And bid me come to Thee.
That with Thy saints I may praise Thee.
Forever and ever. Amen.

WHAT MONEY CAN BUY

Money will buy:
A bed BUT NOT sleep.
Books BUT NOT brains.
Food BUT NOT appetite.

Finery BUT NOT beauty
A house BUT NOT a home.
Medicine BUT NOT health.
Luxuries BUT NOT culture.

Amusement BUT NOT happiness.
A crucifix BUT NOT a Saviour.
A church pew BUT NOT heaven.
What money can't buy,
Jesus Christ can give freely without charge.

Is Jesus Christ your Lord and Saviour? If not, you can get a new lease on life right now.

Confess to God that you have sinned and that you want to turn from your sins to receive Jesus as Lord of your life.

Through that step of believing faith you can start life afresh with your sins forgiven and a new life in Christ.

LIFT UP YOUR HEART

Let not your heart be troubled
Let not your heart despair,
Lift up your prayers to heaven
To a God Who is always there.

He is with you when you waken
Watches over you when you sleep,
Lifts you when you stumble
As you walk on weary feet.

He is with you in your sorrows
When no one seems to care,
Watching waiting loving
To answer every prayer.

The load He'll always lighten
With joy beyond compare,
When you lift your prayers to heaven
To a God Who is always there.

-- Margaret E. McDonald

IF JESUS CAME TO YOUR HOUSE

If Jesus came to your house to spend a day or two
If He came unexpectedly, I wonder what you'd do.
Oh, I know you'd give your nicest room to such an honored Guest,
And all the food you'd serve Him would be the very best.
And you would keep assuring Him you're glad to have Him there
That serving Him in your home is joy beyond compare.

But—when you saw Him coming would you meet Him at the door
With arms outstretched in welcome to your Heavenly Visitor?
Or would you have to change your clothes before you let Him in,
Or hide some magazines, and put the Bible where they'd been?
Would you turn off the radio and hope He hadn't heard,
And wish you hadn't uttered that last, loud, nasty word?

Would you hide your worldly music and put some hymn books out?
Could you let Jesus walk right in, or would you rush about?
And I wonder — if the Savior spent a day or two with you,
Would you go right on doing the things you always do?

91

Would you go right on saying the things you always
say? Would life for you continue as it does from day
to day?

Would your family conversation keep its usual pace,
And would you find it hard each meal to say a
table grace?
Would you sing the songs you always sing, and read
the books you read,
And let Him know the things on which your mind and
spirit feed?
Would you take Jesus with you everywhere you'd
planned to go,
Or would you, maybe, change your plans for just a
day or so?

Would you be glad to have Him meet your very closest
friends,
Or would you hope they stay away until His visit
ends?
Would you be glad to have Him stay forever on
and on,
Or would you sigh with great relief when He at last
was gone?
It might be interesting to know the things that you
would do
If Jesus came in person to spend some time with
you.

IMMACULATE MOTHER, MARY

If I promise to pray daily
The Rosary that you love,
Will it comfort you in some way?
Can I ease your grief somehow,
Can I dry your tears,
Can I make you this solemn vow?

You ask for very little
After all you have done.
You agreed to be the Mother
of God's one and the only Son.
You know well the pain He would suffer,
and you would feel it all.

When His Body torn and bloody
With crown of thorns dug in,
You had to watch in silence
knowing it was for my sin.
You had to watch his suffering
And His loss of dignity.

Most Immaculate Mother, Mary,
What grief you still withstand,
Not only for that time and place
But the pain is felt daily
As we sin in such disgrace.

Most Immaculate Mother, Mary,
Queen of Heaven, let me try
To amend some of the evil
That caused your Son to die.
Let me dry your tears of sorrow
Let me hold your hand in mine —
Let me lift the thorns that crowned Him
And return them to their vine.

94